A Beginner's Guide to Islam

A Beginner's Guide to Islam

1st Edition

ISBN: 9781081224318

Front image by: pexels.com

For more information about conflict resolution of financial and organizational disputes, go to:

www.mediationbip.com

For book related inquiries, contact us at:

mediationbip@gmail.com

Additional publication from the author:

Caring for the Dead in Islam

Both books can be purchased on www.amazon.com

Contents

Introduction

A Beginner's Guide to Islam is a short initiation for non-Muslims about Islam, as well as a refresher for Muslims who are so inclined. It is not intended to cover all aspects of the religion, by topic or in detail. From the mundane to the controversial, some topics have been omitted intentionally and unintentionally. I attempted to cover some of the basic aspects, but leaving the nuances and subtleties within Islamic creed, law and spirituality.

This book should not replace serious and meaningful dialogue with high character Muslims. In many cities throughout North America there are *Masaajid* (plural for *Masjid*, meaning: a Muslim's institution of worship) that conduct classes for new, and not so new Muslims, and they should be sought, in person and/or via the internet. *A Beginner's Guide to Islam* can serve as a supplement to consistent and appropriate learning from an individual. In my opinion, effective learning includes observation, interaction and practice.

While trying to explain Islam, I remind myself of a verse (*ayah*) in the Quran that states: *"You cannot guide everyone you love to the truth; it is God who guides whoever He will: He knows best those who will follow guidance."*[1]

Prophet Muhammad (saw) mentioned: *"Make things easy and do not make things difficult. Give glad tidings and do not frighten people away."*[2] Hopefully this was accomplished.

---

[1] Quran 28:56. The first number(s), to the left of the colon, are in reference to a chapter in the Quran. The second set of numbers to the right of the colon, are in reference to a verse in the respective chapter.
[2] *Sahih Bukhari* (A historical book that mentions some of the *hadiths* of Prophet Muhammad).

Chapter 1

What is Islam and who is a Muslim?

Islam is an Arabic term for submission to the Creator.[3] The Creator is the One who made everything come in to existence, from humans and animals to the sun and moon. The Creator's name in Arabic is *Allah*. Normally after Muslims say His name, we utter *"subhaanahu wa ta 'aala,"* which means: glory be to Him (Allah), the most high. Muslim is an Arabic term for one who submits to the Creator (Allah). Muslims do not worship Prophet Muhammad (saw), Prophet Jesus (as), or any created being. We worship the Creator of them.

The term *Deen* means way of life. *Deen* can be divided in to three (3) sections:

a. *Iman* (beliefs/faith) is centered around six (6) main topics:[4]
    1. Belief in Allah's (God the Creator) oneness. He has no partner, no children and no parents. He is ever living, never dies. He is the first and the last. Hears all and sees all, and has created everything.
    2. Belief in Allah's Angels. Some of them record our deeds, good and bad.

---

[3] This is a non-linguistic definition, that's based off of context. *"Language cannot express the reality of faith, but it can explain what one believes and why* (Yusuf, 2007, pg. 13)."

[4] In this context *Iman* is equivalent to *Aqeedah* (belief system/what binds us to the religion) and *Tawheed* (the Oneness of Allah).

3. Belief in Allah's Messengers and Prophets (from Adam to Muhammad). Normally after we mention a Prophet's name we say *"alayhis-salaam* (as)," which means "may peace be upon him." After mentioning Prophet Muhammad (saw), traditionally we say *"sallallaahu 'alayhi wa sallam,"* which means "may Allah's prayers (honor and elevation in this context) and peace be upon him," abbreviated as: "saw."

4. Belief in Allah's Books of revelation (The Torah, Psalms, Bible and Qur'an[5], etc.).[6]

5. Belief in the Day of Judgment, when everyone will be fairly judged by Allah, for their actions.

6. Belief in fate (*qadr*), the good and the bad of it, and that Allah knows what has happened, is happening and what will happen. And that Allah has given man free will, to do good or bad.[7]

b. *Islam* in this context is defined by the physical activities of our way of life (*deen*).[8] For example: praying 5 times a day, making *hajj* (pilgrimage to Mecca), and paying money annually to the poor (*Zakat*).

---

[5] The Quran is the final revelation from Allah (God), and was sent to Prophet Muhammad, via the Angel Gabriel (*Jibreel* (as)). It was revealed in the Arabic language over a 23 year period, commencing when Prophet Muhammad (saw) was 40 years of age, living in Mecca, during the lunar month of Ramadan.

[6] We believe that the revealed books, other than the Quran, have been tampered with and hence, not in their truest forms.

[7] There are more beliefs for a Muslim, these are just a few.

[8] In this context *Islam* is equivalent to *Fiqh* (Islamic Jurisprudence or Law), not necessarily a religion in general.

4

c. *Ihsan* is the third part of the *deen* that focuses on a commitment to excellent behavior and character building.[9] Having compassion for all humans, eliminating envy and hatred from one's heart, etc.

All three parts of *deen* (*iman, islam* and *ihsan*) are necessary to be a very good, well-rounded Muslim. It is extremely important to avoid being a "cafeteria Muslim."[10] One who picks and chooses which part of the *deen* they will follow, as one would pick certain foods at a lunch counter. *"You who believe, enter wholeheartedly into submission to God (Allah) and do not follow in Satan's footsteps, for he is your sworn enemy."* [11] [12] Therefore, a Muslim should accept the *deen* in its totality. If you struggle with a particular part of the religion, keep struggling and Allah will reward you, *insha'Allah* (God willing).

Remember that some cultural practices are indifferent Islamically, and should not be made to represent Islam based off of Muslims in a given area practicing the said acts for years immemorial. At the same time, there are some cultural practices that are not congruent with Islam, and they should be avoided to the best of one's ability. It can be difficult at times to differentiate between cultural and Islamic practices; however, when you are patient,

---

[9] In this context *Ihsan* (a commitment to excellence/proficiency) is equivalent to *Tasawwuf* and *Tazkeeyah*. All of them essentially focus on being a better human, by purging spiritual diseases from the heart.

[10] This is a term that the author derived from a radio host: Joe Madison 'The Black Eagle,' on SiriusXm radio, the Urban View channel. The radio host actually uses the term 'cafeteria Christians,' but 'Muslims' is applicable as well.

[11] Quran 2:208

[12] It is important to understand that Satan (singular: *shaytaan,* plural: *shayateen*) is a Jinn(s) (an invisible creation of God, some are good and some are bad) and he is real. The evil ones amongst the *shayateen* whisper to mankind to do evil; however, they have no power to make people do bad acts. That's a choice humans solely make.

constantly asking Allah (swt) for guidance and have sincere intellectual curiosity, hopefully things can be made more clear over time.

The Qur'an states:

Struggle for (seeking the pleasure of) Allah, a struggle that is owed to Him. He has chosen you and did not impose any hardship on you in the religion (Deen), the faith of your father Abraham. He (Allah) named you as Muslims (people who submit to the Creator) earlier and also in this (Qur'an), so that the Messenger (Prophet Muhammad) becomes a witness to you, and you become witnesses to (other) people. So establish prayer, pay alms to the poor and hold fast to Allah. He is your patron (advocate). So, how excellent He is as a patron (advocate), and how excellent as a supporter!

(Qur'an 22:78)

Chapter 2

Who was Prophet Muhammad (saw)?[13]

Allah (swt) sent Messengers to guide, give glad tidings (happy news), judge between people and warn those in a particular place at a particular time.[14] [15] Prophet Moses (as) was sent to a people who were skilled in magic, so one of his miracles was a staff (a long, straight stick), which he was able to use for different things.[16] Prophet Jesus (as) was sent to a people who were skilled in medicine, so one of his miracles is that he healed the sick, by the permission of Allah.[17] All of the Prophets came with an overriding monotheistic focus, One God, One Creator, worship Him (Allah). However, the nuances of their messages varied.

The one exception to the above was the final messenger, Prophet Muhammad ibn Abdullah (saw), who was sent to all of mankind, even though his message originally started with a specific group of people. He was born in the Arabian city of Mecca in the 6th century. He was from noble lineage, and often called "the truthful one (Al-Ameen)" before revelation. After receiving revelation from Allah (swt), Prophet Muhammad was persecuted for thirteen (13) years for calling people to worship the One Creator, as Abraham, Moses

---

[13] The following is not intended to be an exhaustive description of his life, just a few sentences to provoke interest. Please refer to the biographies of Prophet Muhammad (saw) for an in depth description of his life. There are many lectures on the life of Muhammad (saw) on youtube.com. Instructor Omar Suleiman does an excellent job explaining such.

[14] With the exception of Prophet Muhammad (saw), he was sent to all of mankind.

[15] Quran 2:213

[16] Quran chapter Ta Ha (20).

[17] Quran 3:49

7

and Jesus attempted to do. So he, along with some of his companions, migrated to a city called Medina (*Yathrib*) partly for religious freedom.[18] While in Medina, Prophet Muhammad designed a constitution, which helped to manage the new community politically. The constitution spelled out the rights and responsibilities of the different groups, Muslim and non-Muslim.[19] By the time he (saw) passed away, he was able to unite practically all of the tribes of Arabia under his guidance.

Prophet Muhammad (saw) had thousands of companions (ra). The word *Sahaabah* is the Arabic equivalent for companions of the Prophet (saw). Two of them are:

- Khadijah bint Khuwaylid (ra): The Prophet's wife, employer, main supporter and first convert to Islam. Together they had 6 children.
- Abdullah ibn Uthman (a.k.a. Abu Bakr Al-Siddiq) (ra): The Prophet's best friend before and after he (saw) received revelation from Allah. Abu Bakr was also the first sovereign political leader (*Khalifah*) of the Muslim community after Prophet Muhammad (saw) passed away.

After mentioning the Companions/*Sahaabah* (ra), traditionally we say *radi-Allahu 'anhum* (may Allah be pleased with them), abbreviated as "ra." The *Sahaabah* (ra) are critical for our understanding of Islam, because they witnessed the character and actions of Prophet Muhammad (saw) directly. Then they passed that information and knowledge of the Prophet (saw) on to

---

[18] This migration was after some of his Companions migrated to Abyssinia (an Eastern section of Africa, land of the Negus (r), due to persecution. In Africa, the Muslims were given religious freedom.

[19] Tahir Ul-Qadri, Dr. Muhammad. (2012). *The Constitution of Medina*. Minhaj-ul Quran Publications PDF version

a group called the *Taabi 'een* (students of the Companions *(ra)*). Then the *Taabi 'een*, passed their knowledge to another group called the *Tabi-Tabi 'een*, which are the students of the students of the *Sahaabah* (ra). Those first three (3) generations of Muslims are considered the righteous predecessors (*Salaf al-Saalih*).[20] Prophet Muhammad (saw) mentioned in two *hadiths* that:[21]

> *The best people are those of my generation (Sahaabah), then those who come after them (Tabi 'een), then those who come after them (Tabi-Tabi 'een)......*
>
> (Bukhari)
>
> Also:
>
> *.....so you must keep to my sunnah (the Prophet's way) and to the sunnah of the rightly guided leaders of the Muslims, those who guide to the right way.*[22] *Cling to it with your molar teeth......*
>
> (Abu Dawud)

---

[20] Some more examples of the *Sahaabah* are: Ali ibn abi Talib, Aisha bint abi Bakr and Bilal ibn Rabiah (ra). Some examples of the *Tabi 'een*: Hasan al Basri, Ibn Sirin and Ibn Jurayj (as). Some examples of the *Tabi tabi 'een*: Malik ibn Anas, Al Shafi'i and Ahmad ibn Hanbal (r).

[21] A *Hadith* is an individual report of an action, instruction or saying of Prophet Muhammad (saw), or his approval, disapproval, or silence regarding some matter or action.

[22] These are the earlier leaders of the Muslim community, directly following Prophet Muhammad's (saw) death. Respectively: Abu Bakr, Umar ibn Khattab, Uthman ibn Affan, Ali ibn abi Talib and Hasan ibn Ali (ra).

Key points:

- *Prophet Muhammad (saw) said: "I have been sent to perfect good character." (Al-Muwatta) Therefore, good character should be a personal and ongoing priority for every Muslim.*
- *Prophet Muhammad (saw) never hit or beat a women or child.*
- *He (saw) never forced anyone to be Muslim. The Qur'an clearly states: "There shall be no compulsion (in acceptance) of the Religion." (Quran 2:256)*

Chapter 3

What is the Shariah?

The *Shariah* is essentially "*the collection of values and principles derived from the Quran and Sunnah that form the moral, religious and legal teachings of Islam.*"[23] A prominent Islamic scholar, Ibn Qayyim al Jawziyyah (r) said:

> Verily the Shariah is founded upon wisdom and welfare for the servants (of the Creator) in this life and the afterlife. In its entirety it is **justice, mercy, benefit and wisdom**. Every matter which abandons justice for tyranny, mercy for cruelty, benefit for corruption, and wisdom for foolishness is not a part of the Shariah, even if it was introduced therein by an interpretation.[24]

The *Shariah* includes many things: the obligation to perform prayer at certain times of the day, fasting the month of Ramadan, respecting and honoring parents, avoidance of lying, a husband providing for their wife, giving charity to the poor, not engaging in gambling, etc. *Fiqh* is different yet sometimes used interchangeably with *Shariah*, and it means Islamic jurisprudence or law. *Fiqh* is more so the scholars interpretation/understanding of the *Shariah*.

Islamic *hudud* (literally: boundaries) laws are under the rubric of Islamic law in general. It delineates the punishments for people who

---

[23] Elias, Abu Amina. (April 18, 2013). "Sharia, Fiqh, and Islamic law explained." Retrieved from, www.abuaminaelias.com

[24] Ibid.

commit theft, the consuming of intoxicants, fornication, adultery and etc.[25] It's important to understand that this aspect of the *Shariah* cannot be implemented by any Muslim other than a Muslim leader (ideally just) in an area under complete Islamic jurisdiction.[26]

Key points:

- *The Shariah encompasses marriage, divorce, financial transactions, prayer, pilgrimage to Mecca, eating habits, etc.*
- *The Shariah does not mean or insinuate "punishment."*
- *The root word for Shariah is shara'a, which means "to start." The linguistic definition for Shariah is "a water hole" or "drinking place." The Islamic technical meaning of Shariah is divine Islamic Law.*

---

[25] For a brief explanation on Islamic criminal law, please refer to: "Stoning and Hand cutting –Understanding the Hudud and the Shariah in Islam" by: Jonathan Brown www.yaqeeninstitute.org

[26] Complete Jurisdiction meaning: the complete control and power of a given area, with total authority over taxes, currency, contracts, government formation, military, etc.

Chapter 4

The five pillars of Islam[27]

Prophet Muhammad (saw) stated:

Islam is built on 5 (pillars), testifying that there is no god but Allah, that Muhammad (saw) is His servant and Messenger, and the establishment of prayer, payment to the poor, pilgrimage to the house (in Mecca), and the fast of Ramadan. (Sahih Muslim)

The first pillar mentioned is the *shahaadah,* which is testifying that there is nothing worthy of worship, except Allah, and that Prophet Muhammad is the last and final messenger. The second pillar mentioned is prayer. Muslims must pray at least 5 times a day with conditions.[28] The third pillar mentioned is almsgiving. Once every fiscal lunar year, Muslims must give to the poor a certain amount of money.[29] Pilgrimage (*Hajj*) to Mecca, is the fourth pillar mentioned and is mandatory on every Muslim at least once in their life, if able. The *Ka'bah* (cube shaped structure) is in Mecca, and was re-built by Abraham (as) and his son, Ishmael (as). The area surrounding the *Ka'bah* is a place of worship (Masjid) and is where some of the rites of *Hajj* are performed. And when Muslims pray, they face the direction of the

---

[27] All of the five pillars have conditions and/or prerequisites. Please consult a local Imam or person of knowledge for more details.

[28] For a detailed description of prayer and the respective times for all 5 prayers, search on the internet for 'Islamic Prayers' or 'description of Salah.' And for the rest of the pillars do the same. Also, go to your local Masjid for guidance.

[29] In some cases, Muslims are to give in 'kind.' For example, a Muslim sheep herder that has a certain number of sheep is to give a predetermined amount of those sheep to the poor.

Ka'bah. The fifth and final pillar mentioned is fasting the whole lunar month of Ramadan. Of course, there are more duties and obligations in Islam. For example: getting married, being good to neighbors, taking care of family, etc. The 5 pillars are essentially the actions that Islam is buttressed on.

Key points:

- **Shahaadah** = *Testification/bearing witness.*
- **Salah** = *Prayer. The five obligatory prayers are: 1. Fajr/ the dawn prayer 2. Zhuhr/ the noon prayer 3. Asr/ the afternoon prayer 4. Maghrib/ the sunset prayer 5. Ishaa/ the late night prayer. Prayer is supposed to be a deep spiritual experience, so try to concentrate, focus and be still.*
- **Zakat** = *Almsgiving. The mandatory giving of 2.5% of your sitting wealth once a year, to the needy.*
- **Hajj** = *Pilgrimage to Mecca. During the 11th Islamic lunar month (Dhul-Hijjah).*
- **Siyaam** = *Fasting. One of the goals of fasting is to learn self-restraint. The mandatory fasting is specifically during the 9th Islamic lunar month called Ramadan, which last 29 or 30 days, based off of a naked-eye moon sighting. Fasting of Ramadan is basically from dawn to sun down, not 24 hours. If one has a medical condition they should seek medical advice. Also, Ramadan is not a holiday. One of the Islamic holidays is the first day of Shawwal, which is the month that follows Ramadan. The holiday is called Eid al-Fitr (The Breaking Fast holiday), which is when Muslims celebrate by praying collectively in large groups, listening to a speech, exchanging gifts, sharing food and etc.*

- *Some of our actions are based on the lunar cycle of the moon, rather than the solar cycle. For instance: fasting, hajj and zakat. With the lunar cycle of the moon, the night comes before the day.*

Chapter 5

How to become a Muslim?

Converting to Islam is a simple process, yet weighty. Normally we call that process "shahaadah." Shahaadah means bearing witness or testifying to the following statements:

> I bear witness that there is nothing worthy of worship, except God (Allah). And I bear witness that Muhammad (saw) is the (last) messenger of God (Allah). [30]

When a person sincerely testifies and accepts Islam (the religion), they are acknowledging all of the attributes of Allah (God): His mercy, ever-forgivingness, His nurturing of mankind, His ever-watchfulness, along with the aforementioned articles of faith. [31] Moreover, one acknowledges Prophet Muhammad ibn Abdullah (saw) as the last and final messenger on earth with a specific message to the world of worshipping the Creator thru good deeds and the eschewing of bad deeds.

To enter Islam, it is not necessary to have witnesses. That is a matter between the individual and Allah. However, initially to be formally recognized and to facilitate in being given certain rights, it is recommended to have Muslims witness the conversion, so there will be no doubt as to the way of

---

[30] The second statement is specifically in reference to Muhammad ibn Abdullah (saw), from the 6th and 7th century Arabia, not any other Muhammad or person. Also, the testimony in whole does not necessarily need to be in Arabic. See www.virtualmosque.com 'Declaration of Faith' article, by Yahya Ederer.
[31] Chapter 1, part A.

life a person has chosen.[32] Further, it is unnecessary to change one's name, first or last, unless it means something abhorrent. Name changing is not an essential part of accepting Islam.[33] By changing one's name, some family members may find it disrespectful and offensive. A person should think carefully before changing their name, and make a decision based off of prayer and consultation.

After becoming Muslim, one should learn how to prepare for formal prayer, which includes: washing the whole body, covering the body, facing the direction of Mecca (*qiblah*) and making sure that no dirty substances are on your person and prayer area.[34]

When one becomes a Muslim by taking their *shahaadah*, they are committing themselves to Allah and the Muslim *ummah* (community). Moreover, they are now clear representatives and ambassadors of the said *ummah*. An ambassador should never display behavior that would be considered detrimental to their country/nation/community; therefore, attempt to act accordingly.

Take some time every so often to learn about the history of Muslims and Islam in your area. Be mindful of the sisters and brothers within your community who have accepted and practiced Islam before you, worked hard and have sacrificed to establish Islam in your locality and country.

Our Lord, forgive us and our brothers (and sisters) who preceded us in faith and put not in our hearts (any) resentment toward those who

---

[32] Example: right to an Islamic burial.
[33] Zarabozo, Dr. Jamal (2017). "A Note on Ibaaddah-Related Practices and the Muslim Convert." PDF
[34] See previous footnote (#33) for more information and go to a local Masjid for assistance and/or seek help from a well-mannered practicing Muslim. For additional help, don't forget the internet. Dirty substances: urine, feces, semen, and etc.

have believed. Our Lord, indeed You are Kind and Merciful. Quran 59:10

$\mathcal{K}ey\ points:$

- The key to being a well-mannered Muslim is to have modesty (haya) and humility (dhul) before Allah (swt), who sees, hears and knows all.[35]
- Obtain a copy of the Quran and read it daily with a sincere and open heart. Avoiding any legal conclusions.
- Enter Islam wholeheartedly (in its totality). Do not pick and choose which part to accept and which part not to accept.
- Never let anyone discourage you from being Muslim; hence, don't hesitate with taking your shahaadah. Anytime is the perfect time to become a Muslim, as long as you believe the shahaadah statement sincerely and free of will.
- You are not doing Allah (God) a favor by being Muslim. Allah's (God) Highness will not diminish if you don't accept Islam and it will not increase if you accept Islam. Acceptance then action is for your own soul. Not for your parents, children, spouse or an Imam (religious leader), it's for your salvation.
- There will be difficulties once a person enters Islam. Be patient with your family, friends, neighbors, classmates and colleagues. And turn to Allah through prayer and getting excellent advice from high character, trusted individuals.

---

[35] Yusuf, Hamza. (N.D.). "Signs, Symptoms and Cures of the Spiritual Diseases of the Heart (PDF)."

19

- *Yes, you have to believe in Jesus (as) to be Muslim! However, we do not believe he was God (Allah) or the son of God. He was a messenger of God.*
- *"If a person accepts Islam, such that his Islam is good, Allah will decree reward for every good deed that he did before, and every bad deed that he did before will be erased........." (Sunan An-Nasa'i)*
- *"A man is upon the religion of his best friend, so let one of you look at whom he befriends." (Sunan al-Tirmidhi)*
- *Avoid extremism. Whether too rigid and strict or too neglectful and lax.*
- *The Quran was revealed in the Arabic language; therefore, make a commitment to learn the language enough to perform the obligatory parts of prayer (salah).*
- *Gradualism (tadarruj) should be employed when applicable.*
- *Avoid being overwhelmed and dogged over Islamic personalities. Focus more on the accuracy of their message.*

Chapter 6

Race and Color in Islam

As we mentioned earlier, Islam is submission to the Creator (Allah); therefore, its message is targeted to all of mankind. Be they white, black, green or brown. Islam is not a black religion, white religion, African, Middle Eastern or Arab religion. Muslims come in all different colors, speaking hundreds of languages and interestingly, most are non-Arabs and non-Arabic speakers.

Further, the idea of race is extremely flawed. It is important to know that:

There is not a single biological element unique to any of the groups we call white, black, Asian, Latino, etc. In fact, no matter how hard people try, there has never been a successful scientific way to justify any racial classification, in biology. This is not to say that humans don't vary biologically, we do, a lot. But rather that the variation is not racially distributed.[36]

Even with its flaws, race and by extension color, are normally used as a way of identifying humans. Recognizing people by color, language or any other non-derogatory descriptions, in a non-discriminatory way, with good intentions, is satisfactory. However, when people use those descriptions to discriminate and act unjustly, is when we have more problems in society.

---

[36] Fuentes Ph.D., Augustin. (2012). "Race is real, but in the way many people think." Psychology Today www.psychologytoday.com

In many parts of the world, traditionally, people would call someone by the language they spoke. So someone would be a Frenchman, because they spoke French, or Arab, because they spoke Arabic, or Fulani, because they spoke Fulani. Those classifications were never meant to indicate color of skin. With the age of "nation building," the concept of people in a given area was made complicated. For instance, the *Sami* people traversed the land directly below the Norwegian and Barents Sea. At some later point however, they were told they were Norwegian, Swedish or Finnish. In many parts of the world, what followed was that nation, language and color of skin did not align; however, some people simplified in a derogatory manner, a way to identify people, which has caused tremendous problems in the world.

Islamically, the first human was Adam (as). In Arabic the root of the word Adam is "a-da-ma," which means to be brown, an intelligent person.[37] Prophet Moses' (Musa (as)) stories are the most mentioned stories in the Quran, and by all Islamic information, he was a dark-skinned man. Prophet Solomon (Sulaymaan (as)) is said to have been a dark-skinned man. His eventual wife, Bilquis (r), was a black woman from east Africa/southwest Arabia. And she was praised in the Quran as a very good leader of a sizeable area. Prophet Abraham's (Ibrahim in Arabic (as)) wife, Hajar (r), was a black woman, and the mother of the Arabs.[38] Moreover, every Muslim must make *Hajj* (the pilgrimage to Mecca) once in their life, and one of the rites that are mandatory to perform imitates her actions from hundreds of years ago, and Prophet Muhammad (saw) is unequivocally from that union, of course many years later. [39] A man by the name of Luqman, is praised in the Quran, and is

---

[37] Omar, Abdul Mannan. (2010). *Dictionary of The Holy Qur'an*. NOOR Foundation – International Inc. (PDF)

[38] Mother of the Arabs before the mixing with Europeans. Hajar and Prophet Abraham had a child named *Ismaa'eel* (Ishmael).

[39] This is in reference to the rite called: *Saa'ee* (walking between the mountains, hills *Safa* and *Marwah*).

opined to have been a black man.[40] Some Islamic sources strongly state that Jesus (Isa (as)) was a dark-skinned man.[41] Ali (ra), Prophet Muhammad's (saw) cousin and the fourth leader (Caliph) of the Muslim community, is said to have been "black-skinned."[42] The first treasurer and caller to prayer for the Muslim community, Bilal ibn Rabah (ra), was a black man. Moreover, amongst the four major schools of Islamic Law (*Fiqh*), two of them, Abu Hanifah (r) and Ahmed ibn Hanbal (r) had a dark complexion.[43] Also, Prophet Muhammad (saw) said, "*I have been sent to all the red and black.*"[44] Arabs generally considered themselves black and all others red. Nevertheless, it is important to remember that all these great figures were not necessarily from the African continent upon their birth; rather, they simply had some degree of a brown complexion.

There's no group of people in Islam that should be looked at as 'token' Muslims, occupying space to placate others. Muslims from all different backgrounds, shapes and colors are significant in their own right. And have meaningfully contributed to the great history of Islam. From Ibn Rushd (Averroes) in Muslim Spain to Mansa Musa, ruler of the Mali Empire, to the Aceh Kingdom in modern day Indonesia.

Islamic sources state that there were 124,000 Prophets.[45] Roughly 25 are specifically mentioned in the Quran.[46] All the unalike humans from Adam

---

[40] Some Islamic scholars dispute whether Luqman was a prophet or a very pious man.

[41] Suleiman, Sheikh Omar. "An incomplete list of black Prophets." Retrieved from, www.youtube.com on February 18, 2019.

[42] According to Ibn Jawzi (r) in *Safwat Al-Safwa*.

[43] "Physical descriptions of the Four Imams." Retrieved from, www.ilmgate.com on February 18, 2019.

[44] Sahih Muslim

[45] Some scholars say that we don't know the exact number. Also, Islam distinguishes between Prophets and Messengers. Prophets were inspired and had communication with God, while Messengers were inspired by God, had communication, and

(as) to Muhammad (saw), was more than likely extremely similar to the people they were sent to. So at the very least, the overwhelming majority of those people were given someone that looked like them and talked like them for guidance. Unfortunately, sometimes when African Americans, people of the global majority (people of color) try to identify with some of the major figures in history, people say "it's not about color or physical descriptions," yet the majority of the depictions of these great figures are Anglo-Saxon white. Why not make them all look "Chinese," "Native American," red-headed or the height of a dwarf, if color and physical descriptions don't matter?

No person is better than another because of their physical description, age, race, gender, income or lineage. Ultimately, Allah (swt) will decide on The Day of Judgment, who was good, and who was bad. However, mainly due to the European slave trade and Colonialism, brown/black complexioned people were and are induced to feel inferior thru culture.[47] The proposed inferiority complex is transferred in a culture via politics, entertainment, magazines, books, religious institutions, and medicine. The darker the shade, the more undervalued, underestimated and marginalized people are.[48]

That being the case, the physical descriptions of the aforementioned people was meant to give comfort, solace and clarity to

---

delivered a specific message to their people. Of course, with the exception of Muhammad (saw), he was sent to mankind, including his own people.

[46] According to some sources.

[47] Examples of marginalized groups: African Americans, *Siddis* in India and Pakistan and the indigenous people of Australia (Aboriginals).

[48] This is an indirect quote from Joe Madison, '*the black eagle*,' heard on Sirius XM's Urban View channel.

those who can use it, not arrogance and hatred for another hue, or a reverse superiority complex for brown/black complexioned individuals.

Prophet Muhammad (saw) said:

...people are all the children of Adam and Adam was created from dust (earth). Allah said: "O people, We have created you male and female and made you into communities and tribes that you may know one another. Verily, the most noble to Allah is the most righteous of you."

(Quran 49:13) (Tirmidhi)

Key points:

- *No group has a monopoly on the religion, whether political, financial, spiritual or educational.*
- *No group has a monopoly on good or bad behavior.*
- *Race or color of skin, are descriptions of appearance, not determinants of character or intellect.*

Chapter 7

Sects, Groups and Unity

On Islam, unity with fellow Muslims is a major theme.[49]

Allah (swt) says in the Quran:

And hold firmly to the rope of Allah all together and do not become divided........ (Quran 3:103)

Verily, those who have divided their religion and become sects, you have nothing to do with them. Their affair is only left to Allah, then He will inform them about what they used to do. (Quran 6:159)

Turn in repentance, be mindful, and establish prayer. Do not be among those who commit idolatry, those who divided their religion and became sects, each party rejoicing in itself. (Quran 30:31-32)

Prophet Muhammad (saw) said:
Do not hate each other, do not envy each other, do not turn away from each other, but rather be servants of Allah as brothers (or sisters). It is not lawful for a Muslim to boycott his brother for more than three days. (Sahih Bukhari) Also, "None of you truly believes, until he loves for his brother what he loves for himself."[50]

---

[49] And to a larger extent, unity with humanity.
[50] Source: Nawwawi 40 Hadith. Also, Imam Nawwawi (r) opined that the word 'brother,' was in reference to 'mankind,' (*Naas*) not just a Muslim brother or sister!

Muslims should avoid all sectarian beliefs and actions.[51] It is a red flag when someone calls you to a group, to engage in practices that are abhorrent to Islam, not consistent with the basic principles of the religion or are cult-like. For example: disparaging your fellow Muslim, believing you or your titled group is better than others, injuring/killing non-Muslims, etc. This does not mean joining mundane (day to day/ordinary) groups or associations are invalid or inappropriate on face value.[52] This chapter simply attempts to shed light on the problem of intentional and malicious division in Islam and the ever-present need for unity.

Division and sectarianism in Islam is real, despite the verses of the Quran warning against such behavior. There have been debates and dialogues with the various groups in and outside of Islam for years. Well intentioned people have tried to bridge the gaps, sometimes successfully, and sometimes unsuccessfully. May Allah reward those who have labored solely for the pleasure of Allah (swt), *amen*.[53] Allah says in the Quran, "*The believers are but brothers, so make reconciliation between your brothers and be conscious of Allah that you may receive mercy.*" (Quran 49:10) If someone has the drive to continue or start new dialogue, excellent. For those who have no interest, there should at least be an understanding of a "circle of cooperation."[54] Meaning, Muslims who hold different views, should be able to work together on significant issues, be they political, financial, security related or educational. Whatever that will benefit humans in general and specifically Muslims, coalescing should be

---

[51] Sectarian: "*caused by or feeling very strong support for the religious or political group that you are a member of, in a way that can cause problems with other groups.*" From Cambridge Dictionary, www.dictionary.cambridge.org

[52] For example: homeschool associations, trade associations, political associations, etc.

[53] *Amen* in this context means: Oh Allah, please answer our prayers.

[54] This was coined by Dr. Yasir Qadhi, from a lecture about sects in Islam.

explored. The Quran states: *"...and cooperate in righteousness and piety, but do not cooperate in sin and aggression..."*[55]

The term *Sunni* signifies a Muslim that tries to follow Prophet Muhammad's (saw) way of life (*Sunnah*), along with the practices of his *Sahaabah* (Companions).[56] When someone accepts Islam by saying *"there is no God, but Allah (the One and Only God), and Muhammad (saw) is the Messenger of Allah,"*[57] they are Muslim, period! When it comes to business transactions, marriage and so on, a person should always do their due diligence by studying the individual to see whether the relationship have the possibility of bearing fruit (financial, emotional, political, etc.), independent of the other party being this kind of Muslim or that kind of Muslim. Moreover, one will always find ultra-conservative, conservative, moderate, liberal and ultra-liberal thinking Muslims within Islam.[58] Each person will gravitate towards the position that they are more comfortable with. Many move between the different classifications depending on the topic. So a person may be conservative when it comes to covering their body, yet liberal when it comes to preparation of their *halal* (permissible) meat.[59]

With all that being said, Prophet Muhammad (saw) never sanctioned, implicitly or explicitly, any form of violence towards groups because of their beliefs or practices that caused no physical harm to others. Individuals and groups should be able to disagree on matters and live peacefully at the same time, they are not mutually exclusive.

---

[55] Quran 5:2

[56] And by extension the *Taabi 'een* (students/followers of the *Sahaabah*) and *Taabi taabi 'een* (students/followers of the students/followers of the *Sahaabah)*. The term *Sunnah* connotes different meanings, and in this context is equivalent to "a path."

[57] This is another way of testifying (taking *shahaadah*).

[58] These classifications are not meant to label Muslims. They are meant to give insight into the complexity of human thinking in general and Muslims specifically.

[59] No one should go around calling themselves or others 'a conservative Muslim' or 'a liberal Muslim.'

Key points:

- *Avoid unnecessary name calling. "O you who have believed, let not men ridicule other men; perhaps they may be better than them; nor let women ridicule [other] women; perhaps they may be better than them. And do not insult one another and do not call each other by [offensive] nicknames. Wretched is the name of disobedience after [one's] faith. And whoever does not repent - then it is those who are the wrongdoers." (Quran 49:11)*
- *Avoid calling yourself anything other than Muslim.[60]*
- *Islam teaches us to bring people together, when appropriate, not divide people unnecessarily.*
- *No group has a monopoly on good or bad behavior.*
- *No group is monolithic.[61] Most of the diversity amongst Muslims is a positive, not a negative.*

---

[60] Of course, there are some exceptions to this statement: democrat, Hanbali, American, Nigerian, millennial, etc.

[61] In this context it means: all thinking one way.

Chapter 8

Sins and Sinners

"All of the children of Adam are sinners, and the best sinners are those who repent." (Tirmidhi)

"All of my Ummah (community of Muslims) will be forgiven except those who sin openly."[62] (Bukhari)

On Islam, we usually differentiate between major and minor sins:

If you avoid the major sins which you are forbidden, We (Allah) will remove from you your lesser sins and admit you to a noble entrance [into Paradise]. (Quran 4:31)

There are a multitude of opinions explaining what constitutes a major sin.[63] Typical major sins are: associating partners with Allah, theft, unjust killing, taking or giving usury/interest, sex while not married (fornication), sex with someone outside of your marriage (adultery), gambling, consumption of intoxicants with no need (recreational marijuana, alcoholic beverages, cocaine, etc.), disobeying/disrespecting parents (Muslim or non-Muslim), slander and backbiting, lying, selling illegal drugs, etc. We will attempt to expound on a few, namely: *fornication/adultery, selling or abusing illegal/legal drugs, disobedience/disrespecting parents* and *homosexuality*.

---

[62] This also includes those who sin privately, but then disclose their actions to the public.

[63] Umarji, Osman. (2011). "Staying away from major sins." Retrieved from, www.virtualmosque.com on February 20, 2019.

Fornication/Adultery

In our tradition, we are commanded to marry when capable. Prophet Muhammad (saw) said:

> *O young men, if you are able to support a wife, then get married. Verily, it restrains the eyes and protects the private parts. Whoever is not able to do so, then he must fast as it is a means of control.* (Bukhari)

Restraining eyes from lustful staring is applicable to females as well.[64] And like any other temptation, it can be difficult. Therefore, we have to be cognizant of the following things:

- Lowering our eyes when necessary. This does not mean we cannot look at the opposite gender. Just not lustfully or at certain parts of the body.
- Some would say that one's eating habits have a lot to do with their sexual appetite. So eating better, which includes eating less and better quality foods, should be incorporated in to our lifestyles or maintained.
- The environment and company we keep can also affect us. One should avoid watching movies, music videos and listening to songs that arouse their sexual drive. Of course pornography is *haram*; moreover, it's important to understand that Islam is not focused on titles at the expense of substance/actions. Therefore, looking at the opposite gender lustfully and/or a naked body, is *haram*.[65] Whether it's called pornography or something else is irrelevant.[66]

---

[64] The Islamic understanding of women covering a certain way has two angles. Women should cover appropriately and men should appropriately lower their gaze. Neither side should worry or focus about the other.

[65] With some exceptions: babies, medical care, etc.

[66] Looking at your Islamically legal spouse, babies and medical necessities, are amongst the exceptions to looking at the same or opposite gender's private parts.

- Fasting should be practiced to help lower the sexual drive as well. Remember, if you have the ability to stay away from food (a basic physical necessity) while fasting, you have the ability to stay away from illicit sex. Difficult as it may be, it is still possible. It is a matter of using your strength in one area, and applying it somewhere else.
- Planning to get married should be done carefully and appropriately. Hence, try not to rush in to marriage. There should be *kafaa'a* (suitability), meaning that the prospective couple should be compatible with regards to their understanding of the religion, personality, finances, health, goals in life and etc.
- Staying or getting active in good deeds is important as well, to help keep your mind off of the prohibited. Help out at a masjid, community center, community garden, nursing home, food bank, etc. Read and pray more.
- Understand that fornication and adultery is prohibited (*haram*). This may seem obvious, but it can be overlooked at times. God will not put any burden on you more than you can bear. You will receive a reward for staying away from the *haram*. When and how, no one knows but Allah.

Selling or abusing Illegal/Legal Drugs

The selling of illegal drugs is unequivocally *haram*. Moreover, the abusing of legal (i.e. prescription) drugs is also prohibited. Recreational marijuana is considered *haram* as well, because of its intoxicating nature and lack of need. Medicinal marijuana, on the other hand, is a very complex subject. There's an Islamic legal maxim, which states: *certainty is never removed by doubt*. This is based on a hadith that calls for Muslims to leave actions that cause doubt for actions that don't cause doubt. Another legal maxim is that *actions are based*

Muslim men should cover their body from navel to knees, at the very least in public. Muslim women should cover their whole body except face, hands and feet (some opinions say that the feet should be covered), at the very least in public. Remember that tight clothes are very similar to no clothes! These descriptions of what to cover and not to cover are termed the '*awrah*' or 'Islamic private area.'

on intentions. These maxims should guide Muslims in the absence of specific Islamic legislation; also, assessing the level of need. Moreover, consulting an Imam, scholar and a Muslim physician should be sought for the use of medicinal marijuana. Prescription drugs when abused are very dangerous as well, so avoid the abusing of any drugs or herbs.

All intoxicants are generally prohibited to consume in Islam without an excuse.[67] The words in Arabic often used for intoxicants are *Khamr* and *Muskir*, which includes: wine, marijuana, beer, angel dust, and etc. We are told:

> *Satan only wants to cause between you animosity and hatred through intoxicants (Khamr) and gambling and to avert you from the remembrance of Allah and from prayer. So will you not desist?* (Quran 5:91)

> *Every intoxicant is Khamr and every intoxicant is forbidden. He who drinks wine (or consumes any other intoxicant unjustifiably) in this world and dies while he is addicted to it, not having repented, will not be given a drink in the Hereafter.* (Sahih Muslim)

Also, the selling of illegal drugs or drugs that should be dispensed thru a physician and pharmacy without a need can be tantamount to spreading corruption on the earth (Arabic: *Fasaad fi al-Ard*).

> *And of the people are some who say, "We believe in Allah and the Last Day," but they are not believers. They [think to] deceive Allah and those who believe, but they deceive not except themselves and perceive [it] not. In their hearts is disease, so Allah has increased their disease; and for them is a painful punishment because they [habitually] used to lie. And when it is said to them, "Do not spread corruption on the earth," they say, "We are but reformers (wholesome people)." Unquestionably, it is they*

---

[67] There are always exceptions. Seek advice from an Islamic scholar.

who are the corrupters (of the earth), but they perceive [it] not. (Quran 2:8-12)

Fasaad is corruption, unwholesomeness or the intentional, significant disturbance of public peace. Many low level drug dealers are therefore involved in *fasaad.* However, we cannot overlook the corruption of some politicians, bankers, employers and religious leaders. They too, are spreading corruption on the earth and can have a far greater negative impact on society than a low level drug dealer. Nonetheless, they are all clearly wrong.

Disobedience/Disrespecting Parents

Allah says in surah *Al-Nisaa*, verse 36:

Worship Allah and associate nothing with Him and be good to parents.

Also:

Your Lord has decreed that you worship none but Him and be good to your parents. Whether one or both of them reach old age with you, do not say to them a word of annoyance and do not repel them but rather speak to them a noble word. Lower to them the wing of humility for them out of mercy and say: My Lord, have mercy upon them as they brought me up when I was small. (Quran 17:23-24)

Prophet Muhammad (saw) said:

Verily, Allah has forbidden you from neglecting your duty to your mothers. (Sahih Bukhari)

Shall I not tell you about the worst enormities (Major Sins)? They are three: idolatry against Allah, disobedience to parents, and false witness. (Sahih Bukhari)

No child can compensate his father unless he finds him as a slave, buys him, and sets him free. (Sahih Muslim)

At no point in any of the aforementioned sources, is there a mention of "Muslim" or "non-Muslim" parents. The guidelines and commands are in reference to parents in general. Whether or not they are Muslim is inconsequential. By logical extension, we should include grandparents, uncles and aunts. Moreover, there is no age limit for being obedient and kind to your parents. Be the person 12, 18, 21, 40 or 65, obedience and treating parents with excellence, even if they treat you poorly, is mandatory. On the other hand, parents should be very careful not to abuse their God-given status, by not overstepping boundaries, requiring that their child do things unreasonable, or asking their child or children to do something illegal and/or un-Islamic.

Homosexuality

Homosexuality is romantic attraction, sexual attraction or sexual behavior between members of the same sex or gender.[68]

In Islam, sexual relations with the same gender falls under the rubric of fornication and/or adultery; therefore, sexual behavior with the same gender is considered *haram* (forbidden). We elected to mention it separately, for clarity sake. Prophet Muhammad (saw) said:

A man is not to look at the 'Awrah (nakedness) of a man, and a woman is not to look at the 'Awrah (nakedness) of a woman. A man is

---

[68] Homosexuality. Retrieved from www.wikipedia.com , February 18, 2019.

not to be alone with a man under one garment, and a woman is not to be alone with a woman under one garment. (Tirmidhi)[69]

Prophet Lot (as) criticized some men for their preference of males over females. *"Do you indeed approach men with desire instead of women? Rather, you are a people behaving ignorantly."*[70] Therefore, we cannot doubt the Islamic position on homosexual behavior.

Interestingly, when someone says that they are gay or a lesbian, do they mean that they are attracted to the same gender and/or are intimate with the same gender? Both are personal matters that there is no need to disclose; hence, are not for public consumption. Some people try to obtain validation for their actions from others, by forcing people to agree with their way of life; however, in Islam, the standard has been set, and anyone who interprets the Islamic legal sources to say that sexual behavior with the same gender is *halal* (permissible), are inaccurate.

All humans go through tribulations/trials/difficulties (*museebah*). For some people, homosexuality may be their trial to overcome. Remember, accepting Islam wholeheartedly is critical to being an excellent Muslim. When one takes their *shahaadah* (testimony) it does not entail perfection. The trials you may have had before accepting Islam do not disappear overnight. One has to consciously work to eradicate their short-comings, which can take years to be rid of. There is no magic bullet, so embrace the process. Prophet Muhammad (saw) said, *"If Allah intends good for someone, then he afflicts him with trials."*[71] For those who are struggling with any trial, calamity, affliction or hardship, the following advice is salient:

---

[69] The *'awrah* for males around other males is everything between the navel and the knees. The *'awrah* for females around other females is navel to knees. However, in our culture, it is advised that women not show the upper parts of their body to anyone with some exceptions: their husbands, infants, necessary medical treatment, etc.
[70] Quran 27:55
[71] Bukhari.

There is no Muslim who is stricken with a calamity (trial) and says what Allah has enjoined – 'Verily to Allah we belong and unto Him is our return. O Allah, reward me for my affliction and compensate me with something better' – but Allah will compensate him with something better.
(Muslim)

Islam accepts all people, regardless of previous actions. However, we cannot attempt to change the religion to everyone's preferences and desires. Rather we should conform to Islamic decorum in order to receive mercy and guidance from Allah (swt). Further, Muslims that are struggling with homosexuality should remember when they go to the Masjid or an Islamic event to observe all proper Islamic manners.[72]

On the other hand, Muslims should be very careful with condemning homosexuality, while being silent on fornication and adultery and other sins. All of them are sinful behavior, despite our personal bad habits and views. We need to be consistent and truthful in rejecting acts that are prohibited, not picking and choosing which to be outraged about.

Allah (swt) mentions in the Quran, "*...there is to be no aggression except against the oppressors.*"[73] Prophet Muhammad (saw) said, "*There shall be neither harm, nor reciprocating harm.*"[74] Consequently, Muslims should never harm anyone because of their sexual preferences or private acts.[75] We are not people overseers or supervisors. "*Part of the perfection of one's Islam is his leaving that which does not concern him.*"[76]

---

[72] For example: men not imitating women in any manner.
[73] Quran 2:193.
[74] Nawwawi 40 Hadith.
[75] Private acts that are legal in American law.
[76] Ibid.

Repentance

Along with the aforementioned sins, the following *hadith* can be used as an additional barometer, when applicable:[77]

> *Righteousness is in good character and morality, and sinful conduct is that which wavers in your soul, and which you dislike people finding out about.* (Hadith from: Bulugh Al-Maram)

This is not to say that if one has no shame, then the act does not constitute a sin. Instead, it points to the normal feelings people have deep down when they err. However, these feelings of course, can be altered by customs and personal habits. So the 'barometer' should be used after explicit Islamic law.

As we mentioned earlier, entering Islam does not immediately purge one from all their previous habits. Nor does it mean that if you were born Muslim (in a non-technical sense) there's no need to ask Allah for forgiveness. Prophet Muhammad (saw) said: *"Turn oh people in repentance to Allah and beg pardon of Him. I turn to Him in repentance a hundred times a day."*[78] If the Messenger sought forgiveness at least 100 times a day, and he was the best of mankind, it follows that we should be in the habit of seeking forgiveness for our sinful acts, knowingly and unknowingly, throughout the day.

Anytime of the day someone can repent for their transgressions by simply asking Allah for pardon.[79] Traditionally one would make a two unit

---

[77] Applicable in that, some scholars have opined that humans do not know exactly which sins are major or minor. Allah (swt) have kept them (major sins) hidden, so we should attempt to avoid all sinful behavior, instead of focusing on a specific list.

[78] Sahih Muslim

[79] Don't wait for some special time.

prayer, then after concluding it, one would ask for forgiveness.[80] [81] True repentance includes the following:

1. Immediately stopping the sinful act. One cannot truly be repenting, while still engaged in the sinful act.
2. Sincerely asking for Allah's forgiveness, from the bottom of one's heart. This includes regret.
3. Intending to never commit the act again. Don't promise or vow, just firmly intend![82]
4. Redress any wrongs that were committed to others while engaging in the sin. For example, if a person stole money from someone and did the first 3 steps, but not the last (redressing), how could they have truly repented, when they never returned the money to the rightful owner? In addition, try to perform some kind of act of kindness after committing a sin, perhaps it will help. *"Charity extinguishes sinful deeds just as water extinguishes fire."*[83]

No one is perfect, new Muslim or old Muslim, so we need to turn to Allah (swt) at all times, especially when we have slips and omissions. Satan will whisper to you to give up, "God won't forgive you," "you're too far gone." When you are whispered to, say: *I seek protection with Allah from the accursed Satan.* Remember that Satan wants you to ultimately despair from Allah's mercy.

And when My (Allah) servants ask you concerning Me - indeed I am near. I respond to the invocation of the supplicant when he calls upon

---

[80] There are some special and specific supplications to make when one has committed a sin. Please consult those books that explain such, and/or consult a local Imam on *Salah Al-Tawbah* (prayer of repentance).

[81] The two units (*rak'ah*) would be done in a state of ablution (*wudu*).

[82] In Islam, formally promising and/or vowing to do something has many legal ramifications.

[83] Ibn Majah

Me. So let them respond to Me [by obedience] and believe in Me that they may be guided. (Quran 2:186)

Be conscious of Allah wherever you are. And follow up a bad deed with a good one to wipe it out. And behave well towards people. (Tirmidhi, Nawwawi)

We cannot engage in sinful behavior and expect good outcomes and blessings. If you are doing good deeds, continue. If you are doing bad deeds, attempt to stop and don't compound it with other bad deeds. Most humans do some good and some bad, so hopefully our good acts will outweigh our bad conduct. May Allah forgive us and pardon us for all of our flaws and mistakes, intentionally and unintentionally, *Ameen.*

Key points:

- When you sin, ask Allah ASAP to forgive and pardon you, and follow the previously mentioned steps. If you are addicted to any sinful behavior, admittance is the key to turning things around. Then strive to get legitimate and appropriate help.
- "Whoever increases his prayers for forgiveness, then Allah will grant him relief from every worry, a way out from every hardship, and provide for him in ways he does not expect."(Musnad of Ahmed)

Chapter 9

Jihad

Jihad in Arabic means *"to exert one's self to the extent of one's ability and power, whether it is by word or deed."*[84] Its root is *jahada*, which means "to struggle" or "to exhaust."[85]

> *Jihad is therefore, far from being synonymous with war. Its meaning as war undertaken for the propagation of religion is unknown to the Arabic language and Islam. Imam Bukhârî in his Book of Jihad has several chapters speaking of simple invitation to Islam........... This fact indicates that up to the time of Bukhârî (194-256 A.H.) the word Jihad was used in the same sense as is used in the Holy Qur'an...... Fighting in defense of faith received the name of Jihad because under some circumstances it become[s] necessary for the truth to live and prosper, if fighting had not been permitted, truth would have been uprooted.....*[86]

The Quran says: *"Fight in the way of Allah those who fight you, but do not transgress. Verily, Allah does not love transgressors."*[87] So the purpose of this type of *jihad* is to defend oneself from aggression. Ibn Taymiyyah (r) states:

> *As for the transgressor who does not fight, then there are no texts in which Allah commands him to be fought. Rather, the unbelievers are only fought on the condition that they wage war,*

---

[84] Omar, Abdul-Mannan. (2010). *Dictionary of The Holy Quran*. Noor Foundation International Inc.
[85] Ibid
[86] Ibid. Page 106
[87] Quran 2:190

as is practiced by the majority of scholars and as is evident in the Book and Sunnah.[88]

The aforementioned is concerned with the lesser-*jihad*, while the greater/more important-*jihad* (struggle) encompasses many categories:[89]

a. Striving against the soul (lower self)
b. Struggling against yourself in the obedience of God
c. Teaching good things in the Masjid
d. Speaking the truth in front of a corrupt ruler (leader)
e. Serving one's parents
f. Helping a widow in need
g. Helping the poor
h. Struggling to perform religious obligations (prayer, fasting, etc.)
i. Making *Hajj* (pilgrimage to Mecca)

*Jihad in Islam refers to the spiritual struggle against sin, the struggle to educate and improve our communities, and an armed struggle in defense of the oppressed. **Jihad does not refer to a holy war, because war in Islam is never holy; rather, war in Islam can only be just or unjust.**[90]*

There are several instances of Prophet Muhammad avoiding unnecessary physical confrontations. One example is when his fellow townsmen, the Quraysh, planned to kill him for spreading Islam. And he migrated to Medina instead of fighting the aggressors head-on. Another is when those same aggressors travelled to Medina, and the Muslims under the direction of Prophet Muhammad, made a ditch/trench around the city, effectively avoiding a head-on clash. The Quraysh, not being able to get pass the trench, subsequently returned home. However,

---

[88] Elias, Abu Amina. (2016). "Is there offensive jihad in Islam?" Retrieved from, www.abuaminaelias.com, on March 2, 2019.
[89] Ibid
[90] Ibid

sometimes physical confrontation cannot be avoided and it is necessary to protect oneself and/or family. This is the case with the Battle of *Badr* and *Uhud*, which the Muslims participated in.[91]

Currently, the country with the largest population of Muslims is Indonesia. It was not due to 'forced-conversion,' that the people initially accepted Islam, it was through trade relations. India, Pakistan, Bangladesh and Nigeria round-out the top 5 Muslim populated countries in the world.[92] One would need to explain why people have accepted Islam throughout the world without war or coercion. Needless to say, free will and sincerity was attached to the multitude of reasons that people converted to Islam.[93] Islam in America has grown substantially from 2.35 million Muslims in 2007 to 3.45 million in 2017.[94] Specifically for African Americans, it has many attributes that's appealing, from being tied to a great civilization, having a fraternal spirit, to its basic creed of one God.[95] For Hispanic-Americans, it appears that a connection with Islamic Spain and the structure of worship are amongst the main reasons for conversion.[96]

To reiterate, struggle (*jihad*) is not synonymous with 'killing people.' And struggle can take many forms as mentioned above. *Jihad al-Nafs* or struggling against the soul is the most important form of struggle.

---

[91] *Badr* and *Uhud* are just two examples of the battles that Prophet Muhammad (saw) and some of his companions fought in.

[92] *The Future of World Religions: Population Growth Projections* (PDF). (April 2, 2015). Retrieved from www.pewforum.org

[93] Some would say that people who convert to Islam are in actuality reverting to Islam, because every person is born with the natural inclination (*fitrah*) to submit to God; hence, Islam (submission).

[94] Mohamed, Besheer. (January 3, 2018). New estimates show U.S. Muslim population continues to grow. Retrieved from, www.pewresearch.org.

[95] Jackson, Sherman A. (2005). *Islam and the Blackamerican*. Oxford University Press, Inc.

[96] Padgett, Tim. (October 12, 2013). "Why so many Latinos are becoming Muslims." Retrieved from, www.icna.org

Of course, there have been some over-zealous and violent Muslims throughout history.[97] Logically, we shouldn't maximize the minimum, nor paint an entire group of people with a broad brush. Some of those same violent people have exacted violence against their fellow Muslims. However, there is nothing inherent in Islam that insinuates or leads people towards violence. Some people have an inclination to violent behavior for many reasons, so the vehicle for acting out their aggression could be any: religion, marriage or authority. Allah (swt) candidly mentions in the Quran: *"There shall be no hostility (or aggression) except against aggressors."*[98]

Prophet Muhammad stated:

I witnessed a pact of justice in the house of Abdullah ibn Jud'an that was more beloved to me than a herd of expensive red camels. If I were called to it now in the time of Islam, I would respond.[99]

This was a pact termed *'Hilf al Fudul,'* or 'Pact of the Virtuous.' it began when a business person from Yemen conducted a sale with a Meccan buyer. However, the Meccan buyer did not pay the agreed upon price for the goods, while keeping the product. The Yemeni businessman subsequently appealed to the Quraysh leaders in Mecca for justice. A pact was created which supported victims of oppression, rather than the oppressor, and Prophet Muhammad was one of the signatories.[100] This event was before he (saw) received Quranic revelation. It was organized and ratified by Prophet Muhammad and non-Muslims. Another indication that insight to justice does not originate with Muslims, its origins are from God. And He (swt) can give that insight to whomever he pleases. Moreover, it speaks to the Islamic understanding of universal equity.

---

[97] As well as from other religious and non-religious people.
[98] Quran 2:193
[99] www.abuaminaelias.com
[100] The signature was not by signing of names on a piece of paper. It was through other means, as a signature is: *something that serves to set apart or identify*.

Allah does not forbid you from being kind and just with those who do not fight you because of religion and do not expel you from your homes. Verily, Allah loves those who act justly. (Quran 60:8)

Chapter 10

Who is a Kaafir?

In Arabic the word *Kaafir* denotes someone who has not uttered the *shahaadah* (testimony of faith) or rejects the *shahaadah*. *Kaafir's* Arabic root is *kafara*, which means to cover up.[101] Linguistically *kaafir* can be defined as a farmer, because he "covers up seeds." Also, a branch of *kafara* is *kaffaarah*, which is used in the Quran as expiation of sins, as expiation "covers up" one's sins.

A *kaafir* can consist of:

1. Those who don't believe outwardly (by taking their *shahaadah*) and are not aggressive towards Muslims and Islam.
2. Those who reject Islam outwardly, but are not aggressive towards Muslims and Islam.
3. Those who dislike Islam and believers, but are not aggressive towards Muslims and Islam.
4. Those who actively oppose and fight against Muslims and Islam.[102]

Thus, in general, a *kaafir* is one who does not believe in the *shahaadah* for various reasons respectively. So it's a catchall term that needs specificity depending on who it's addressed to. As Muslims, we should focus

---

[101] Wehr, Hans. (1976). *A Dictionary of Modern written Arabic*. Spoken Language Services, Inc.

[102] Rabbani, Faraz. (2016). "Are all non-Muslims deemed 'kafir'?" Retrieved from, www.seekersguidance.org on March 25, 2019. *Kaafir* can also connote a person who says that they're Muslim, yet disbelieves in their heart, i.e. the *munaafiqun* (hypocrites).

on the outward conduct of people, while leaving the true inner realities to Allah. Accordingly, if a person is a Muslim outwardly, yet inside their heart they reject Islam, that's between them and Allah. If a person appears to be a *kaafir* (in any way) outwardly, yet accepts Islam in their heart, that's between them and Allah. Prophet Muhammad (saw) said, *"I have not been ordered (by Allah) to search the hearts of the people or cut open their bellies."* [103]

Unfortunately, sometimes we use the term *kaafir* too loosely and in a derogatory manner, even though the term can simply signify a non-Muslim. Prophet Muhammad said, *"Beware of harsh and profane words."*[104] Other terms for non-aggressive non-Muslims are:

a. *Ahlul-kitaab* - People of the book (scriptures), specifically Christians and people of the Jewish faith who believe in God. *"They are not (all) the same; among the People of the Scripture is a community standing (in obedience), reciting the verses of God during periods of the night and prostrating (in prayer). They believe in God and the Last Day, and they enjoin what is right and forbid what is wrong and hasten to good deeds. And those are among the righteous. And whatever good they do - never will it be removed from them. And God is all-knowing of the God-conscious."* (Quran 3:113-115)

b. *Insaan* or *Naas* - Mankind. *"Indeed, We created man (insaan) from a sperm-drop mixture that We may try him; and We made him hearing and seeing."* (Quran 76:2)

During the time of Prophet Muhammad, there was a non-Muslim man by the name of Mut'im ibn Adi. Mut'im helped stop the unjust boycott in Mecca against the Muslims. He also instructed his sons to physically protect Prophet Muhammad from the aggressors amongst the

---

[103] Amatullah. (December 27, 2008). "Who are you to judge?" Retrieved from, www.muslimmatters.org
[104] Source: Sahih Al-Bukhari

Quraysh (a powerful group in Mecca), that intended to inflict harm on him. He never accepted Islam, yet after the Battle of *Badr*, the Muslims had prisoners of war, and Prophet Muhammad mentioned that if Mut'im was alive, he would forgive them (the prisoners) for his (Mut'im) sake.[105] Contrastively, Prophet Muhammad's uncle, Abu Lahab, was obstinate and hostile towards Islam and Muslims. It would be dangerous for Muslims to equate all non-Muslims to Mut'im ibn Adi, because there are some people who are actively trying to destroy the lives of Muslims and hate Islam. However, Muslims cannot equate all non-Muslims to Abu Lahab either, because there are some people who are very kind and helpful towards Muslims and don't hate Islam. It's reasonable to assume that both types are prevalent in most areas of the world.

Instead of finding a specific Arabic word or label for a certain person or group, we should call them by their individual names and/or self-proclaimed names.[106] Nobody would like to be called anything derogatory or disrespectful, even if it's true. *"None of you truly believes until he loves for his brother what he loves for himself."*[107] Imam Nawwawi (r), in his explanation of the previous *hadith*, opined that Prophet Muhammad (saw) meant 'brother' in humanity, which includes non-Muslims that are not aggressive towards Islam and Muslims.

---

[105] Tabassum. (2018). 3 Non-Muslims Praised by Prophet Muhammad. Retrieved on April 22, 2019, from www.aboutislam.net
[106] When appropriate.
[107] Source: Imam Nawwawi collection of Hadith.

Chapter 11

Positive religious interactions

People from disparate religions have interacted successfully for hundreds of years in divergent areas of the world, on the personal level and on the national level. The following are three brief illustrations.

In the middle of the 19th century (1847-1852) Ireland was going through 'The Great Famine.' At this moment in history, Ireland was under the rule of England, and predominantly a country of Christians. The Ottoman Empire (a Muslim controlled empire) was being led by Sultan Khaleefah Abdul-Majid. He sent aid in the form of money, to the people of Ireland in their time of need. Also, it is said that he sent three to five ships, full of food to the north east of Ireland. Subsequently, the Irish gave thanks.[108]

Earlier, we mentioned that Prophet Muhammad (saw) was persecuted in Mecca, thus he migrated to Medina. However, before he personally left his home town, some of his companions migrated to a Christian area called Abyssinia.[109] Prophet Muhammad (saw) made it clear that the Abyssinian king was known for his justice. Hence, the Muslims migrated and stayed in Africa, in peace, for a period of time. Eventually the King, Najashi, accepted Islam, and Prophet Muhammad performed the Janazah (funeral) prayer for him, while in Medina.[110]

---

[108] Little known tale of generous Turkey aid to the Irish during the great hunger. (July 6, 2019). Retrieved from, www.irishcentral.com

[109] East Africa, including modern day Ethiopia.

[110] Mohammed, Najeeb. (June/July 1997). The haven of the first hijra (migration). Retrieved from, www.soundvision.com

In 2018, the Tree of Life synagogue in western Pennsylvania was unfortunately attacked, resulting in 11 people being murdered. The Islamic Center of Pittsburgh started a crowdfunding page to raise funeral expenses for the victims. They initially intended to raise $25,000, they eventually collected $190,000.[111]

The aforementioned examples were just to elucidate that religious people can and do interact peacefully. Religions are not the problem. It's the individuals that use them as a tool for hateful acts. Likewise, people can use their respective religion as a tool to extend good.

---

[111] Sadeque, Samera. (October 30, 2018). U.S. Muslims raise $190,000 for burial of Jewish Pittsburgh victims. Retrieved from, www.haaretz.com

Chapter 12

Is Religion necessary?[112]

Some may say that religion has wreaked havoc on the earth. From Islamic terrorism to the Christian crusades to sexual predators in the Catholic Church. On the surface, the opening statement has merit. However, when we remove a few layers, we find that religions are used as a tool for violence and have been for time immemorial, and are not the culprits. Further, the top five (5) deadliest wars known in human history were not initiated by any religious group(s):

1. World War Two (1939-1945) had **85 million deaths**.

2. The Mongol invasions (13th and 14th centuries) had **55 million deaths**.

3. War of Three Kingdoms in China (2nd and 3rd centuries) had **38 million deaths**.

4. Qing conquests in China (17th century) had **25 million deaths**.

5. Chinese Civil War (1850 to 1864) had **25 million deaths**.[113]

The Mongol invasion was perpetrated mainly against Muslims. With regards to the Chinese civil war, the non-religious government officials were

---

[112] The origin and meaning of the term 'religion' is debated. In this chapter, the term 'religion' is used as a systematic way of life that authentically originated from Allah to a Messenger.

[113] Kiprop, Joseph. (September 10, 2018). "What was the deadliest war in history?" Retrieved from, www.worldatlas.com

persecuting a religious group, so the religious group fought back, and a war ensued.

In the book *Dying to Win*, Robert A. Pape explains the rare relationship between suicide attacks and religion:

> I have compiled a database of every suicide bombing and attack around the globe from 1980 through 2003 – 315 attacks in all..... The data show that there is little connection between suicide terrorism and Islamic fundamentalism, or any one of the world's religions. In fact, the leading instigators of suicide attacks are the Tamil Tigers in Sri Lanka, a Marxist-Leninist group whose members are from Hindu families but who are adamantly opposed to religion. This group committed 76 of the 315 incidents, more suicide attacks than Hamas. Rather, what nearly all suicide terrorist attacks have in common is a specific secular and strategic goal: to compel modern democracies to withdraw military forces from territory that the terrorists consider to be their homeland. Religion is rarely the root cause, although it is often used as a tool......[114]

---

[114] Pape, Robert A. (2005). *Dying to Win*. Random House, New York.

Some may ask, if there is a God, why would he or she allow all this destruction on earth and all these children to suffer? *"He (God) is not questioned about what He does, but they (humans) will be questioned."*[115] Why would humans, as the stewards and inheritors of the earth, cause such destruction after receiving guidance from Allah (God)?[116] We mentioned in a previous chapter that one of the reasons God sent Messengers, was to lead humans to better conduct and character. Without those Messengers and Prophets, we would be in a worse situation. In his paper on the environment, Jihad Brown, quoting from Imam Ghazali (r), explains that the four qualities of good character are wisdom, temperance, courage and justice, which are internal realities. And he also stated:[117] *It is when the inner constitution* (or inner qualities of character) *of the steward is in a state of imbalance and disequilibrium that disruption, disharmony and disaster appears in the extra-mental (existing outside the mind) environment.*[118] [119]

The Quran states:

Calamities have appeared on land and sea because of what the hands of the people have earned, so that He (Allah) makes them taste some of what they did, in order that they may return (to the right way). (Quran 30:41)

---

[115] Quran 21:23

[116] Guidance and understanding can come in many forms: revelation and instruction, via Prophets, admonition from another person, advice, a true dream, studying history, and being precautionary with others.

[117] From Al Ghazali (r).

[118] Brown, Jihad. (November 3, 2013). Metaphysical Dimensions of Muslim Environmental Consciousness. Retrieved from, www.tabahfoundation.org

[119] The non-italicized words are from the author of this book.

Interestingly, some people are spiritual but not religious, meaning that they are not part of any organized or systematic religion. It's an old question: how does one determine right from wrong? Does man have the ability to decipher all good and bad solely with their intellect? Islamically, the very essence of revelation was to quell arguments, give good news, guide and warn. And if mankind was left without guidance there would be countless practices throughout the world, each person would have a specific interpretation of what's right and wrong. It's true, that some religious people have given religion a bad name. However, we shouldn't throw the baby out with the bath water. The dynamics of any group is that individuals will emerge as leaders. One of the main attributes of a good leader is their ability to influence and persuade others. Therefore, direction from a leader is inevitable within any society. The question is: who will you allow to give you direction and guidance? For Muslims, its Prophet Muhammad (saw).

In reference to humans attacking or injuring other humans, remember, that some of us are a test for others:

We did not send any messengers before you (Prophet Muhammad), but all of them used to eat food and walk in the markets. And We have made some of you a test for some others. Would you observe patience? And your Lord is Ever-seeing." (Quran 25:20)

All that is needed for turbulence to be prevalent in any society is for enough good people to be silent about the people who cause harm to others. Prophet Muhammad said:

Whoever among you sees evil should change it with his hand. If he is unable to do so, then with his tongue. If he is unable to do so,

58

then with his heart, and that is the weakest level of faith. (Sahih Muslim)

Also, the turmoil we see in the world has been predicted by the Messenger (saw):

Verily, my community will be afflicted by the disease of communities."
They (companions) said, "O Messenger of Allah, what is the disease of
communities?" The Prophet said, "Insolence (rude behavior), hubris
(pride), turning their backs to one another, competing for worldly
possessions, hating each other, and miserliness (being cheap/stingy),
until there will be oppression and then there will be bloodshed.[120]

In the face of adversity, we should maintain the doing of good. *"If the*
Resurrection (Day of Judgment) were established upon one of you while he
has in his hand a sapling (young tree), then let him plant it."[121] Thus, being optimistic about the future, while going through trials and tribulations is a quality we should integrate in to our identity. Moreover, Muslims should take solace in the following:

Those who believe, and do deeds of righteousness, and establish
regular prayers and regular charity, will have their reward with their
Lord: on them shall be no fear, nor shall they grieve.[122]

Humans clearly need guidance from The Creator (Allah), and throughout history that guidance came in the form of Messengers and Prophets, which led to religious systems. Prophet Muhammad ibn Abdullah

---

[120] al-Mu'jam al-Awsat by: Al-Tabarani.
[121] Musnad of Ahmad
[122] Quran 2:277

was the last and final Messenger sent to mankind, to practically show us how to interact with the Creator and His creation.

Conclusion

Expectantly, you are more interested in Islam as a way of life. If you are not Muslim, and have an inclination towards Islam, pronounce the *shahaadah* with conviction, sincerity and free will. Then practice Islam wholeheartedly to the best of your ability. If you are someone who has already uttered the *shahaadah*, remember your duty to Allah and act correspondingly to your beliefs.

O you who have believed, why do you say what you do not do? How despicable it is in the sight of Allah that you say what you do not do! (Quran 61:2-3)

Our Lord, grant us good in this world and good in the Hereafter and save us from the punishment of the Hellfire. (Quran 2:201)

O Allah, bring our hearts together, reconcile between us, guide us to ways of peace, and deliver us from darkness into light. Keep us away from immorality, outwardly and inwardly, and bless us in our hearing, our seeing, our hearts, our spouses, and our children. Accept our repentance, for you alone are the Relenting, the Merciful. Make us grateful for your blessings, praising and accepting them, and give them to us in full. (Sunan Abu Dawud)

Bibliography

Al-Tabarani. (n.d.). *al-Mu'jam al-Awsat.*

Amatullah. (December 27, 2008). Who are you to judge? Retrieved from,

www.muslimmatters.org

Brown, Jihad. (November 3, 2013). *Metaphysical Dimensions of Muslim*

Environmental Consciousness [PDF version]. Retrieved from,

www.tabahfoundation.org

Brown, Jihad. (April 9, 2018). Stoning and Hand cutting-Understanding the Hudud

and the Shariah in Islam. Retrieved from, www.yaqeeninstitute.org

Elias, Abu Amena. (n.d.). Sharia, Fiqh, and Islamic law explained. Retrieved from,

www.abuaminaelias.com

Faraz, Rabbani. (2016). *Are all non-Muslims deemed 'kafir'?* [Audio file]. Retrieved

from, www.seekersguidance.org

Fuentes Ph.D, Augustin. (2012). Race is real, but in the way many people think.

Retrieved from, www.psychologytoday.com

Hackett, C., Cooperman, A., Ritchey, K. (April 2, 2015). *The Future of World Religions:*

Population Growth Projections, 2010-2050 [PDF Version]. Retrieved from

www.pewforum.org

Holy Quran

Homosexuality. In *Wikipedia*. Retrieved April 22, 2019, from www.wikipedia.com

Ibn Majah

Jackson, Sherman A. (2005). *Islam and the Blackamerican*. Oxford University Press,

Inc.

Kiprop, Joseph. (September 10, 2018). What was the deadliest war in history?

Retrieved from, www.worldatlas.com

Little known tale of generous Turkey aid to the Irish during the great hunger. (July 6,

2019). Retrieved from, www.irishcentral.com

Madison, Joe (Radio Host). (n.d.) *The Joe Madison show*. [Radio Broadcast].

Washington, D.C. Sirius XM Broadcasting.

Mohamed, Besheer. (January 3, 2018). New estimates show U.S. Muslim population

continues to grow. Retrieved from, www.pewresearch.org

Mohammed, Najeeb. (June/July 1997). The haven of the first hijra (migration).

Retrieved from, www.soundvision.com

Musnad of Ahmad

Nawwawi 40 Hadith

Omar, Abdul Mannan. (2010). *Dictionary of The Holy Qur 'an*. NOOR Foundation –

International Inc.

Padgett, Tim. (October 12, 2013). Why so many Latinos are becoming Muslims.

>	Retrieved from, www.icna.org

Pape, Robert A. (2005). *Dying to Win*. Random House, New York.

Physical descriptions of the Four Imams. (n.d.). Retrieved from, www.ilmgate.com

Sahih Bukhari

Sahih Muslim

Sadeque, Samera. (October 30, 2018). U.S. Muslims raise $190,000 for burial of

>	Jewish Pittsburgh victims. Retrieved from, www.haaretz.com

Sectarian [Def. 1]. In *Cambridge Dictionary* online, retrieved May 1, 2019, from,

>	www.dictionary.cambridge.org.

Suleiman, Sheikh Omar. (July 26, 2016). *An incomplete list of black Prophets* [Video

>	file]. Retrieved from, www.youtube.com.

Sunan Abu Daud

Tabassum. (2018). 3 Non-Muslims Praised by Prophet Muhammad. Retrieved from,

>	www.aboutislam.net

Tahir Ul-Qadri, Dr. Muhammad. (2012). *The Constitution of Medina* [PDF version].

Tirmidhi

Umarji, Osman. (2011). Staying away from major sins. Retrieved from,

>	www.virtualmosque.com

Wehr, Hans. (1976). *A Dictionary of Modern written Arabic*. Spoken Language

   Services, Inc.

Yusuf, Hamza. (2007). *The Creed of Imam Al-Tahawi*. Zaytuna Institute.

Yusuf, Hamza. (n.d.). *Signs, Symptoms and Cures of the Spiritual Diseases of the Heart*

   [PDF version].

Zarabozo, Dr. Jamal. (2017). *A Note on Ibaadah-Related Practices and the Muslim*

   Convert [PDF version].

Made in the USA
Middletown, DE
08 June 2021